Simply *in* Season
Children's Cookbook

Mark Beach
Julie Kauffman

Herald Press

Scottdale, Pennsylvania
Waterloo, Ontario

Library of Congress Cataloging-in-Publication Data
Simply in season children's cookbook : a world community cookbook / by Mark Beach
and Julie Kauffman.
p. cm.
ISBN 0-8361-9336-9 (hardback : alk. paper)
1. Cookery--Juvenile literature. I. Beach, Mark. II. Kauffman, Julie.
TX652.5.S54 2006
641.5'622--dc22   2006023565

This cookbook is part of the World Community Cookbook Series commissioned by
Mennonite Central Committee (MCC) to promote the understanding of how the food
choices we make affect our lives and the lives of those who produce food.
MCC is a relief, community development, and peace organization of the Mennonite and
Brethren in Christ churches in Canada and the United States. www.mcc.org

The publisher and the authors have made every effort to emphasize the importance of
safety procedures when children are cooking in the kitchen. Neither the publisher nor the
authors can assume responsibility for any accidents, injuries, losses, or other damages
resulting from the use of this book. Children should not use this cookbook without adult
supervision.

SIMPLY IN SEASON CHILDREN'S COOKBOOK
Copyright © 2006 by Herald Press, Scottdale, Pa. 15683
            Released simultaneously in Canada by Herald Press,
            Waterloo, Ont. N2L 6H7. All rights reserved
International Standard Book Number: 0-8361-9336-9
Library of Congress Catalog Card Number: 2006023565
Printed in Canada

Cover and book design: Julie Kauffman
Photography: Jenna Stoltzfus
Food stylist: Cherise Harper
Additional photography: Melissa Engle, Brenda Burkholder, bigstockphoto.com

15 14 13 12 11 10   10 9 8 7 6 5 4 3

To order or request information, please call 1-800-245-7894
or visit www.heraldpress.com.

ENVIRONMENTAL BENEFITS STATEMENT

Mennonite Publishing Network saved the following
resources by printing the pages of this book on
chlorine free paper made with 10% post-consumer
waste.

TREES	WATER	SOLID WASTE	GREENHOUSE GASES
2 FULLY GROWN	998 GALLONS	61 POUNDS	207 POUNDS

FSC
Mixed Sources
Cert no. SW-COC-001271
© 1996 FSC

Calculations based on research by Environmental Defense and the Paper Task Force.
Manufactured at Friesens Corporation

acknowledgments

This cookbook, like the food we eat, required many hands to seed, cultivate, nurture, and prepare. The inspiration sprang from the original *Simply in Season* cookbook whose authors Mary Beth Lind and **Cathleen Hockman Wert** spent two years gathering recipes and stories about how the food choices we make affect our lives and the lives of those who produce food.

Each recipe selected for *Simply in Season Children's Cookbook* was tested by children and parents alike. Thanks to Emma and Calvin with mom Jackie Mullin; **Noah** and **Sophie** with mom **Lori Bergey**; Alex and his mom Kimberly Smart; **Audrey** and **Wesley** with mom **Naomi Beach**.

This endeavor would never have taken wings without the dedication of several members of the Mennonite Central Committee Communications Department who did research, gathered fun facts, and assisted with photography: Marla Pierson Lester, **Rosa Pérez Perdomo**, Barbara Wiebe, and **Melissa Engle**.

Any cookbook made for children requires a mirror image of themselves. So thanks to our models Kelly Aksu, **Olivia Bortner**, Justin Geisenberger and **Tatiana Hill** each of whom spent the better part of a day patiently dipping their fingers into batter, stirring drinks endlessly and grating carrots just one more time, all in an effort to show their peers how it's done. Special thanks also to photographer Jenna Stoltzfus and food stylist **Cherise Harper**.

And finally, without the creative ideas, engaging design, and collaboration of Julie Kauffman, this cookbook would have remained somewhere in a file of projects to work on someday.

Instead that someday is today. Enjoy this cookbook, your children, and the food you prepare and eat together.

—**Mark Beach**

spring

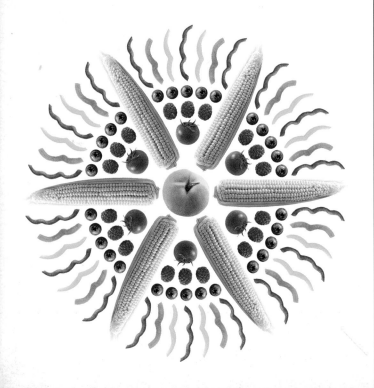

summer

contents

autumn

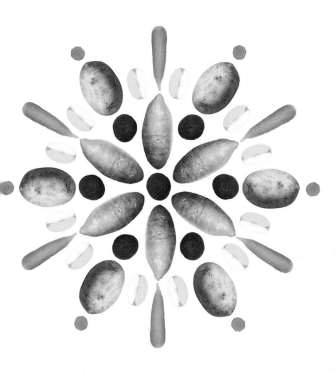

winter

greetings

"Would you like a piece of chocolate cake with coconut icing?"
I ask my neighbor. He smiles and graciously accepts the cake of
mud topped with grass clippings. "Mmm, that's pretty good," he
says before taking me for a ride in the wheelbarrow. Later in the
kitchen, I help my mother shell and freeze peas from our garden.
Food and play, food and imagination, food and art, food and even
some responsibility were all part of my childhood.

As a dietitian, I often work with children. My favorite job is
to offer tasting parties as a way to encourage and educate about
good food and nutrition. Moving children from "ugh!" to "mmm!" is
so rewarding. And *Simply in Season Children's Cookbook* just made
that move easier with its creative ideas and recipes.

Today, faced as we are with an epidemic of overweight
children whose idea of vegetables is often french fries and ketchup,
it is time we redeem food from the hands of multinational
corporations and cartoon commercials. It is time to put food, real
food, into the hands of children and let them play.

Simply in Season Children's Cookbook is an imaginative,
active way to invite kids of all ages but especially 6 to 12 year olds
to get in touch with real food, to see where it comes from, to take
responsibility for preparing it, and to have fun in the process.
Simply in Season Children's Cookbook promotes whole foods in a
whole life experience—from growing foods to growing kids!

I bet my childhood neighbor would prefer a bowl of real
Strawberry Dream Cream to an imaginary piece of chocolate cake
with coconut icing. Let's go make some for him and one for us!
Beat you to the kitchen! Ready, set, eat …

Mary Beth Lind
Co-author of *Simply in Season* cookbook

11 easy steps

to fun cooking and eating.

1. Wash your hands.
2. Put on your apron.
3. Gather ingredients and equipment
4. Wash and dry fruits and veggies.
5. Follow the recipe (with adult help).
6. Smell the aromas.
7. Set the table.
8. Serve the food.
9. Give thanks.
10. Enjoy the meal.
11. Clean up.

Each season this cookbook takes you out to the

garden

into the

kitchen

and around the

table

to enjoy fresh food.

It's about eager hands reaching into the soil, planting seeds and later picking ripe strawberries ready to eat. Each "in the garden" spread shows fruits and vegetables you might find growing in spring, summer, autumn, and winter. Use the chart in the back of the cookbook to document how your garden grows. Also there you'll find a guide to starting your own herb garden.

It's about messy gooey hands, flour scattered across the counter and the sweet smells of Very Berry Crunch wafting from the oven. Each recipe—drawn from the original *Simply in Season* cookbook—was kid-tested and parent-approved, with modifications to meet adventurous and picky eaters alike. Sorry, we took the parsnip recipe out.

It's about proud hands placing bowls of freshly made Green Monster Soup on the table as family and friends gather around. Each season ends with a prayer of thanks to God for the gift of food and for all the hands involved in bringing it to the table. Recite these prayers or create your own blessings.

We admit we don't cover it all. But we do hope this cookbook opens your eyes, nose, and curiosity to the food around you. Go ahead. Get your hands into it.

spring

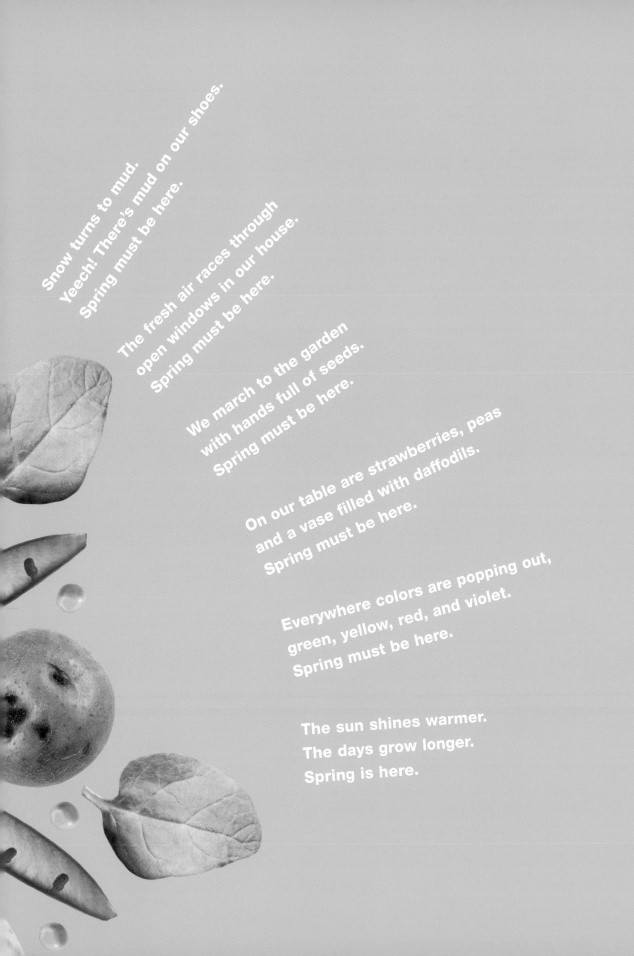

Snow turns to mud.
Yeech! There's mud on our shoes.
Spring must be here.

The fresh air races through
open windows in our house.
Spring must be here.

We march to the garden
with hands full of seeds.
Spring must be here.

On our table are strawberries, peas
and a vase filled with daffodils.
Spring must be here.

Everywhere colors are popping out,
green, yellow, red, and violet.
Spring must be here.

The sun shines warmer.
The days grow longer.
Spring is here.

spring in the garden

time to plant

As the air warms, move container plants outside in the sun during the day, but still bring them in at night.

Prepare your garden. Rake away leaves and debris that collected over the winter and loosen the soil. Dig holes and plant seeds or transplant seedlings you started indoors. Water them well.

When colors begin to pop out of the ground, invite friends over and have a first sprout party.

Tools you will need:

- gardening gloves
- rubber boots
- heavy-duty rake
- leaf rake
- shovel
- trowel
- watering can or hose
- materials to make plant signs

mint

Likes to hang out ... page 14
in tea or lemonade, with new potatoes or peas, on salads, or with lamb.

Grows up ...
in a pot on the windowsill or in the garden. Mint can grow as high as 2 feet or 60 cm and spreads quickly. Be careful or it will take over the whole garden.

Spearmint gets its name from the shape of its leaves— like spears.

Ready, set, eat ...
just before it flowers. Leaves should be strong and fragrant, not droopy.

pea

Likes to hang out ... page 17
alone, in salad, in casseroles with rice, in stir-fries and soup or chicken pot pie.

Grows up ...
on a vine-like plant. Round leaves and curly tendrils appear first, followed by white or purple blossoms. The flowers fall off to reveal tiny pea pods. Each pod starts out flat and gets rounder as the peas inside get bigger.

Ready, set, eat ...
when bright green and crisp. The peas inside should be glossy, crunchy, and sweet. Snow peas and sugar snap peas have edible pods that should snap, not bend.

Finding a pea pod with only one pea inside is a symbol of good fortune.

new potato

Likes to hang out ...  *(page 18)*
baked with herbs, in salad with mayonnaise and mustard, or in hot, creamy soup.

Grows up ...
underground beneath a green, bushy plant with heart-shaped leaves. Dug up when very new or young with thin skins.

Potatoes are 80% water.

Ready, set, eat ...
when the flowers drop off the plant. New potatoes should be firm and smooth with no green soft spots. Keep for only a week.

baby spinach

Likes to hang out ... *(page 21)*
with cheese and eggs in quiche, in salad with strawberries, on sandwiches or in dips.

Grows up ...
above ground. Bright green spinach leaves are one of the first vegetables to peek out of the ground after a long winter.

Spinach and other green veggies help you see better.

Ready, set, eat ...
when leaves are tender and perky, not wilted or bruised. Stays fresh only a few days.

straw-berry

Likes to hang out ... *(page 22)*
alone right off the stem, on cereal or ice cream, in jam, atop salads, or in bread or pie.

Grows up ...
wild or in the garden on plants with jagged leaves and white blossoms. Tiny berries start out white and turn red as they ripen. Strawberries like sunny days and cool nights.

Strawberries are a member of the rose family.

Ready, set, eat ...
when plump and bright red with no white or green patches. Size is not important.

Other fruits and vegetables often found in spring:
asparagus, leeks, lettuce, radishes, rhubarb, wild greens

Orange Minty

Makes 2 quarts (2 L)

1
5-6 sprigs fresh mint (each 6 inches or 15 cm long)

Pluck rinsed mint leaves from the stem.
Set aside.

One pound of mint can flavor 135,000 sticks of gum.

2
3 cups water (750 ml)

Pour water in a saucepan.
Bring water to a boil.
Carefully remove saucepan from heat.
Add mint to saucepan and put the lid on.
Let sit 15 minutes or longer.
Remove mint with a strainer or slotted spoon.

3
1/3 cup sugar (75 ml)

Add sugar to saucepan and stir until dissolved.
Set aside to cool.

4
2 cups orange juice (500 ml)
1/2 cup lemon juice (125 ml)

Pour juices into a half-gallon (2-L) serving pitcher.
Add mint and sugar mixture.

5
water and ice

Add enough water and ice to fill the pitcher.
Stir well and serve.

Peas Please

1

2 cups snow peas or sugar snap peas (375 ml)

Remove stems.
Snap peas into bite-size pieces.
Set aside.

2

1 tablespoon ginger root
1 tablespoon oil

Peel and finely chop ginger root.
Heat oil in large frypan over medium high heat.
Add ginger.
Cook and stir about 1 minute.
(Ginger should be fragrant.)
Add sugar snap peas to frypan.
Cook and stir until crisp-tender, about 3 minutes.

3

2 cups peas (500 ml)
3 tablespoons orange juice

Add peas and orange juice to frypan.
Cook and stir until hot, about 2 minutes.
Remove frypan from heat.
Serve immediately.

Peas are an ancient food—they have been found in Egyptian tombs.

17

Potato Crunchers

Serves 3-4

1 Preheat oven to 375F (190C).

2
¹/₃ cup olive oil (75 ml)
1 teaspoon dried thyme
1 teaspoon dried sage
1 large clove garlic (minced)
³/₄ teaspoon salt
¹/₂ teaspoon pepper

Combine in a large plastic container with lid.

3
16 small red or white new potatoes

Wash and scrub potatoes. Pat dry.
Add potatoes to container with herb mixture.
Put lid on tight and shake potatoes to coat well.
Put potatoes on a large oiled baking sheet.
Bake in preheated oven for 20 minutes.
Remove from oven and turn potatoes over.
Bake another 20 minutes.
(Potatoes should be crusty brown on the outside.)
Transfer potatoes to a shallow bowl and serve.

Green Cheese Squares

Serves 4-8

1 Preheat oven to 350F (180C).

2
3 eggs
1 cup milk (250 ml)
1/2 cup whole wheat flour (125 ml)
1/2 cup flour (125 ml)
1 teaspoon baking powder
1 teaspoon salt

Stir together in a large mixing bowl.

Researchers at MIT have used spinach's ability to convert sunlight to energy into an electronic "spinach sandwich" device that may one day power laptops and cell phones.

3
2 cups cheese (500 ml)

Shred cheese.
Add to dough in mixing bowl and stir.

4
3 ounces fresh baby spinach (125 g)
Tear spinach leaves into small pieces.
Add to mixing bowl and stir.
Pour mixture into a greased square baking pan.
Bake in preheated oven about 30-35 minutes.
(A knife inserted in the center should come out clean.)
Cut into squares and serve.

Options: Try adding browned sausage. For thinner snack squares, cut the recipe in half.

Strawberry Dream Cream

Makes 2 quarts (2 L)

1

2-3 cups strawberries (500-750 ml)

Remove stems from strawberries.
Use a fork to mash strawberries in a bowl. Set aside.

2

(This step works best if mixing bowl and beaters are chilled 15 minutes in freezer beforehand.)

2 cups whipping cream (500 ml)

Pour whipping cream into a large, deep mixing bowl.
Beat with electric mixer until soft peaks form.

3

1 1/4 cups sweetened condensed milk (300 ml)
1 cup cold water (250 ml)
6 tablespoons sugar
1/2 teaspoon vanilla
1/4 teaspoon salt

Add with mashed strawberries to whipped cream.
Beat with electric mixer.
Pour mixture into a 9 x 13-inch (3.5-L) pan.
Freeze until mushy, 3-4 hours.
Remove from freezer and put back into mixing bowl.
Beat with electric mixer until smooth but not melted.
Spoon into popsicle containers or return mixture to pan.
Freeze another 3 hours.

Strawberries are the only fruit with seeds on the outside.

around the table

For these days of warmth
We give thanks to God.

For this food upon our table
We give thanks to God.

For our family and our friends
We give thanks to God.

For all the gifts of spring
We give thanks to God.

Amen.

summer

Summer is all around,

sunny sky above and earth below.

Let's run through grass and fields

chasing, shouting, laughing, catching fireflies.

Gather 'round the picnic table

filled with luscious colors,

red tomatoes from the garden,

yellow corn fresh from the field.

Gather 'round the summer table

bright with ripened fruits,

peaches picked from orchard trees,

juicy melons from the vine.

Gather 'round the family table

mother, father, sister, brother.

Friends from near and far arrive.

Summer is all around.

summer in the garden

time to feed and weed

Water and weed your plants while you watch them grow. Water early in the morning before the sun is too hot. Pull weeds out by hand or use gardening tools to help.

Mulch your garden all summer long to keep weeds out and moisture in. Clip your plants (called deadheading) as needed so all their energy can go to producing yummy fruits and vegetables.

Treat yourself to fresh tomatoes, green beans, and berries as they ripen.

Tools you will need:

- gardening gloves
- clippers
- shovel and trowel
- watering can or hose
- gathering basket
- rake
- posts and string to keep plants upright

basil

Likes to hang out ... *pages 35, 36*
with tomatoes, in salads and pasta dishes. (It's what gives pesto sauce its green color.)

In ancient Rome, young maidens would wear a sprig of basil in their hair when they wanted to date.

Grows up ...
into a bushy plant in the garden or in a container. If you see blossoms, cut them back to encourage the plant to grow more. It likes lots of sunshine— don't you?

Ready, set, eat ...
when leaves are firm, not too soft or droopy. Cut basil sprigs with scissors just above any leaf. Now smell it.

cilantro

Likes to hang out ... *pages 35, 36*
in salsa, salads and dips. In Mexican, Asian and Middle Eastern food.

Grows up ...
in pots outside or on a sunny windowsill, or in the ground. Cilantro is the name for the round, jagged leaves of the coriander plant. The stems, roots, and seeds are called coriander.

Ready, set, eat ...
when leaves are young and bright green, not wilting. The tender stems can also be used in fresh or cooked dishes.

Cilantro is actually a member of the carrot family.

28

bell pepper

pages 35, 36

Likes to hang out ...
In salads, on pasta, with other raw veggies as a snack, or stuffed with rice and meat.

Grows up ...
above ground on a green bushy plant. Bell peppers start out green, then change colors and sweeten as they ripen. That's why red, yellow, orange, and even purple peppers are usually sweeter than green peppers.

> Red bell peppers have nine times more vitamin A than green bell peppers.

Ready, set, eat ...
when firm, shiny, and brightly colored without any brown or soft spots. A pepper should feel heavy for its size.

sweet corn

pages 32, 35

Likes to hang out ...
on the cob with butter, paired with peas, in salads and soups, or in cornbread, of course.

Grows up ...
on a long stalk with long flapping leaves. The stalks can grow taller than most adults. If your parents or grandparents grew up on a farm, ask if they ever got lost in a cornfield.

> An average ear of sweet corn has about 800 kernels in 16 rows.

Ready, set, eat ...
when kernels are plump and milky. Look for ears with bright green, snugly fitting husks and golden brown silk.

tomato

pages 35, 36

Likes to hang out ...
alone or in a sandwich, in sauce with spaghetti, on pizza, in salsa, ketchup, soups, and stews.

Grows up ...
on a bush-like plant. Yellow blossoms signal the coming fruits. Tomatoes start out green and turn red as they ripen. Some are the size of grapes. Others are as big as baseballs.

> There are more than 10,000 varieties of tomatoes.

Ready, set, eat ...
when richly red and fragrant. Should feel firm but soft, not squishy. Tomatoes should feel heavy for their size. Never store tomatoes in the refrigerator—the cold kills the flavor.

green bean

Likes to hang out ... (page 36)
alone, with pasta and parmesan cheese, or in casseroles, soups and salads.

zucchini

Likes to hang out ... (page 36)
with other veggies on the grill or in a stew, with dip, stuffed and baked, or in brownies.

eggplant

Likes to hang out ... (page 36)
grilled in sandwiches, in dips, or baked with tomato sauce and parmesan cheese.

Grows up ...
on a bushy plant with heart-shaped leaves and white or purple blossoms. Vining types need long poles or fences to climb.

> **Green beans are also nicknamed snap beans or string beans.**

Ready, set, eat ...
when crisp and brightly colored with a velvety skin. The ends should snap off easily. Avoid mushy tips.

> **In Italy, zucchini flowers (fiori di zucchine) are dipped in batter and fried for a crunchy sweet snack.**

Grows up ...
almost overnight. As the plant grows, fine, prickly hairs will cover the underside of leaves and stems. Then blossoms will give way to bursting zucchinis.

Ready, set, eat ...
when young and tender, small to medium size. Skin should be shiny and firm, not wrinkled or soft.

Grows up ...
on a bushy plant that has roundish leaves with a peak of purple on the edges and deep lavender blossoms.

Ready, set, eat ...
when bright, firm and smooth with no soft or brown spots. Should be heavy for its size.

> **Eggplants were once called "mad apples" because they were believed to cause insanity. It was untrue.**

rasp-berry

Likes to hang out ... (page 39)
alone, in pastries and jams, in salad dressings, or with a kiss of whipped cream.

A raspberry is made up of many individual sections of fruit (called drupelets), each with its own seed.

Grows up ...
to be red, black or golden on the canes of a very prickly plant. Watch your fingers.

Ready, set, eat ...
when brightly colored, plump and round. Choose berries that aren't flattened or leaking juice. The best berries have a hazy, soft gloss. Handle carefully, they're delicate.

blue-berry

Likes to hang out ... (page 39)
alone, with other fruit in salads, in pancakes and muffins, or in pies, tarts and crisps.

Grows up ...
on bushes. Blueberries won't ripen once they're picked.

Ready, set, eat ...
when firm and round with a deep purple-blue skin. Berries should be firm and round, not shriveled.

Early American colonists boiled blueberry skins with milk to make gray paint.

peach

Likes to hang out ... (page 40)
alone, grilled with pork or chicken, in pies and smoothies, or with tapioca pudding.

Grows up ...
on a tree with white blossoms. The trees need cool weather during the winter so they can make peaches in the summer.

Ready, set, eat ...
when soft but not mushy. Let your nose guide you. Ripe peaches should smell sweet. Avoid peaches with large, flattened bruises or with green around the stem.

In China, peaches are a symbol of good luck.

Other fruits and vegetables often found in summer:
cucumbers, melon, okra, plums, cherries

Corny Cornbread

1 Preheat oven to 350F (180C).

2
2 cups cornmeal (500 ml)
1/4 cup honey (60 ml)
1 teaspoon salt
1 teaspoon baking soda

Combine ingredients in a large mixing bowl.

3
3 eggs

Crack eggs into a small bowl.
Beat well.
Add eggs to large mixing bowl.

4
2 cups milk, yogurt, or combination (500 ml)
2 cups corn (500 ml)

Add to mixing bowl and stir together.
Pour into greased 3-quart (3-L) casserole dish or mini bread pans.
Bake in preheated oven 40 minutes.
(Toothpick inserted in center should come out clean.)
Cut into wedges and serve.

Stoplight Salad

1

Handful of fresh basil or cilantro

Snip or tear rinsed leaves into small pieces.

2

1 green bell pepper
2 cups tomatoes (500 ml)
2 cups corn (500 ml)
2 cups cooked black beans (500 ml)

Chop bell pepper and tomatoes into fine pieces
(or use whole grape tomatoes).
Combine with corn and beans in bowl.
Stir in cilantro or basil.

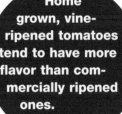

Home grown, vine-ripened tomatoes tend to have more flavor than commercially ripened ones.

3

1 clove garlic
2 tablespoons olive oil
2 tablespoons lime juice

Peel and finely chop the garlic.
Whisk with oil and juice in small bowl.
Pour over salad.
Salt and pepper to taste.
Toss gently and serve.

Option: Can be used as a filling for quesadillas. Put a few spoonfuls in a tortilla with shredded cheese and cook on a griddle.

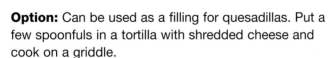

Garden Bobs

Note: If using wooden skewers, soak at least 30 minutes in water before using to prevent scorching.

1

2 tablespoons fresh basil
2 tablespoons fresh cilantro
3 tablespoons olive oil
1/2 teaspoon salt
1/4 teaspoon pepper
1-4 cloves garlic

Snip herb leaves into small pieces.
Peel and finely chop garlic.
Mix all ingredients in a bowl. Set dressing aside.
(For a quick option, try Italian dressing instead.)

2

8-10 cups fresh vegetables of choice: zucchini, cherry tomatoes, bell peppers, green beans, eggplant, onions, mushrooms

Chop into chunky bite-size pieces.
Put half of vegetables and dressing in plastic container.
Put lid on tight and shake to coat vegetables.
Repeat with rest of vegetables and dressing.
Thread a variety of vegetables onto each skewer.
(If you want, add bite-size chunks of meat.)
Grill over medium heat until vegetables are tender.
Serve in wraps, over cooked pasta, or with wild rice.

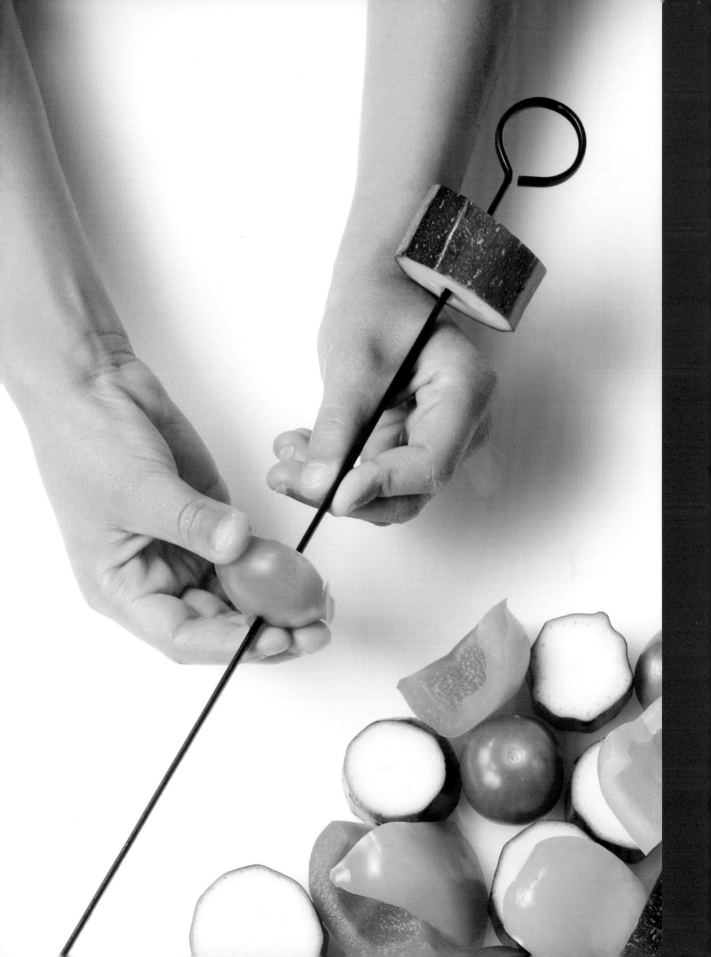

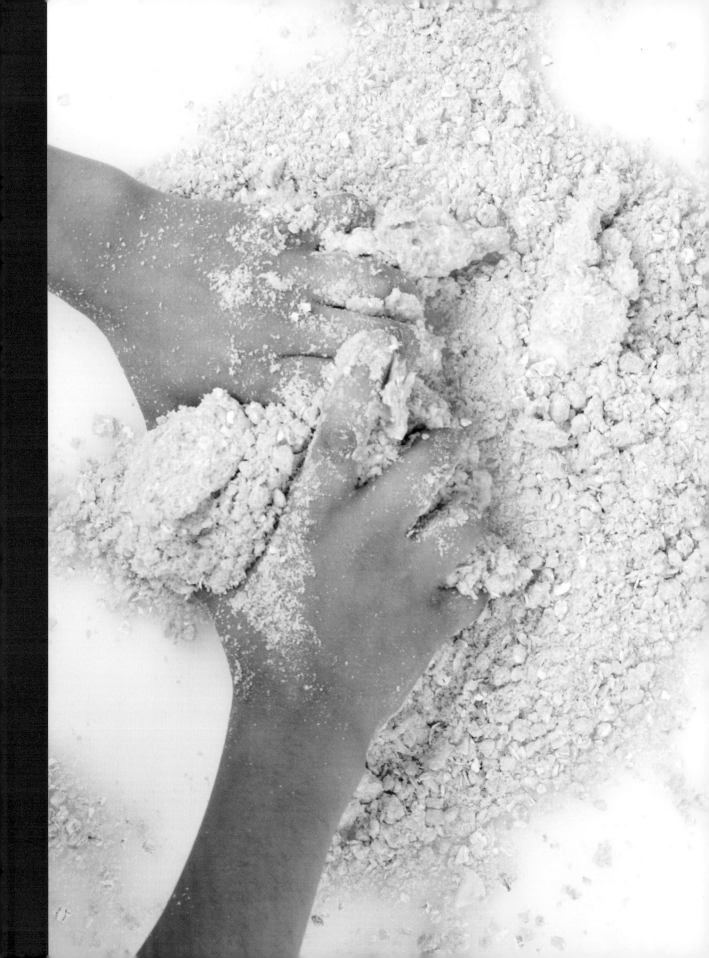

Very Berry Crunch

Serves 8

1 Preheat oven to 375F (190C).

2 **6 cups fresh berries** (1.5 L)**: raspberries, blueberries, blackberries, boysenberries, huckleberries, saskatoons, mulberries**

Combine berries in a large bowl.
Dust lightly with a spoonful of flour and gently mix.
Pour into 9 x 9-inch (2.5-L) baking pan.

3 **3/4 cup flour** (175 ml)
3/4 cup rolled oats (175 ml)
3 tablespoons butter
2 tablespoons oil
2/3 cup brown sugar (150 ml)
1/3 cup chopped nuts (75 ml) (optional)

Mix together with hands until crumbly.
Sprinkle topping over fruit.
Bake in preheated oven about 30 minutes.
(Fruit should bubble and top should be golden brown.)
Serve warm with ice cream, yogurt or whipped cream.

Peachy Smoothie

1

2 cups peaches (500 ml)

Cut peaches in half and remove stone from center.
Peel and cut in half again.
Purée in a blender.

2

1¹/₂ cups vanilla yogurt (375 ml)
1 cup milk (250 ml)
2-4 tablespoons honey or sugar, to taste

Add and blend until smooth.
Pour into glasses and serve.

Options: For a thinner smoothie, replace yogurt with
milk. Instead of peaches, try melon or berries or a
combination of fruits.

around
the table

Before us Lord,
Your bounty spread,
We thank you for this food.

Family, friends,
And neighbors new,
We thank you Lord for all.

Amen.

autumn

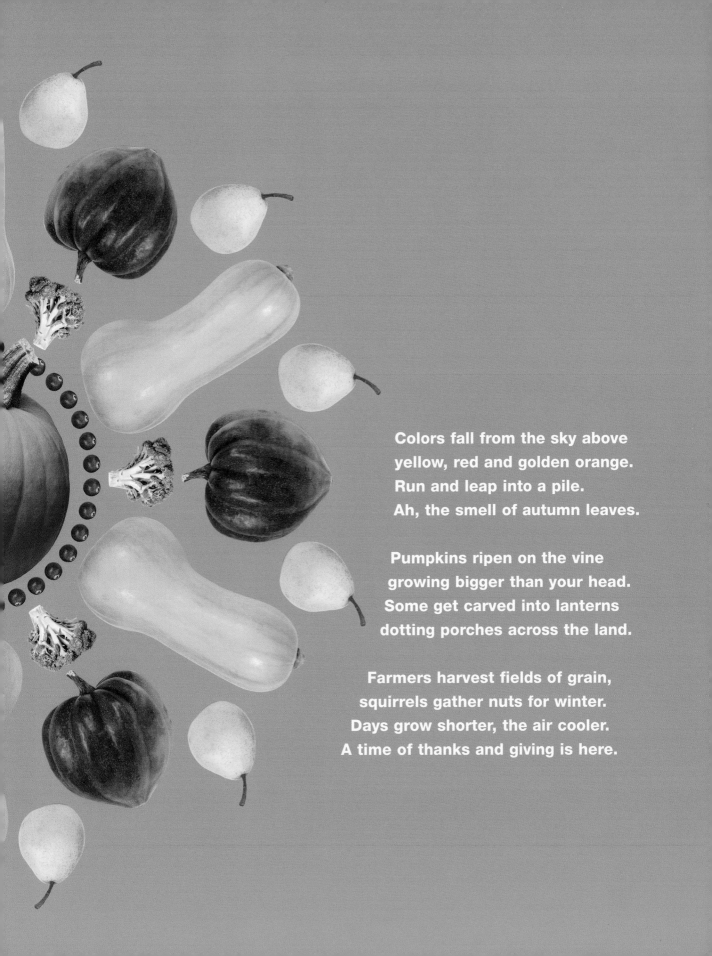

Colors fall from the sky above
yellow, red and golden orange.
Run and leap into a pile.
Ah, the smell of autumn leaves.

Pumpkins ripen on the vine
growing bigger than your head.
Some get carved into lanterns
dotting porches across the land.

Farmers harvest fields of grain,
squirrels gather nuts for winter.
Days grow shorter, the air cooler.
A time of thanks and giving is here.

autumn in the garden

time to harvest

In early fall there are still fruits and vegetables to be harvested. Enjoy digging the last of the potatoes and pulling pumpkins off their vines.

After frost, pluck any remaining green tomatoes, slice them, coat them with seasoned flour, and fry them up for a treat.

Now it is time for the garden to rest. You can leave it be for the winter or mulch some of the dying plants by turning them back into the ground for nourishment.

Tools you will need:

- gardening gloves
- clippers
- gathering basket
- rake
- shovel

broccoli

Likes to hang out ...

(page 51)

with dip, in soup and salad, in stir-fries, or steamed and topped with lemon butter or cheese.

Grows up ... on a plant with big green leaves. It is harvested before its flower buds open. Both broccoli and cauliflower are members of the cabbage family.

> Roman farmers called broccoli "the five green fingers of Jupiter."

Ready, set, eat ... when it is a deep, strong green, not yellowish. Buds should be tightly closed and the leaves crisp. Look for thin stems that are a lighter green than the buds.

pumpkin

Likes to hang out ...

(page 48)

in muffins and bread, in soup either hot or cold, in cheese-cake, and don't forget pie.

Grows up ... on a rambling vine with big green leaves and orange trumpet-shaped flowers. You'll find prickly hairs on the stems and leaves.

> Native Americans used to dry strips of pumpkin and weave them into mats.

Ready, set, eat ... when brightly colored and rock-solid. Choose a pumpkin with the stem still attached. Some pumpkins are especially for making pies and roasting seeds. Smaller ones are better for cooking.

squash

butternut
acorn

Likes to hang out ...
cooked with butter and brown sugar or syrup, in soups and stews, or stuffed and baked.

pages 52, 55

pear

Likes to hang out ...
alone, on a plate with cheese, in green salads, or in pies and other baked desserts.

page 56

cran-berry

Likes to hang out ...
in breads and baked desserts, with apples in pie, or in sauce on a Thanksgiving table.

page 56

Squash seeds can be eaten, ground into paste, or pressed for vegetable oil.

Grows up ...
on a vine. Butternut squash look like large pears with long necks. Acorn squash are shaped like— you guessed it—acorns.

Ready, set, eat ...
when hard with a dull, not shiny skin. The stem should still be attached. Choose large butternuts with a small bottom and a long neck. Winter squash can be stored in a cool, dark place for 3-6 months.

Grows up ...
on a tree with pink blossoms. Pears like warm days and cool nights. They are one of the few fruits that don't ripen on the tree.

Pear trees have been known to grow as old as 300 years.

Ready, set, eat ...
when firm and well-colored. Choose pears that are fragrant and don't have bruises or soft spots.

Grows up ...
on low, scrubby plants in huge, sandy bogs. Bogs are wet and spongy and usually have moss growing in them.

Ready, set, eat ...
when bright or dark red. Pale ones were picked too early and may be sour. Choose berries that aren't too wet or mushy.

Cranberries are also called bounceberries because ripe ones bounce. They also float.

Other fruits and vegetables often found in autumn: brussels sprouts, cauliflower, grapes, persimmons

Pumpkin Minis

Yields 48 mini muffins

1 Preheat oven to 350F (180C).

Pilgrims made their first pumpkin pie by filling a hollowed out shell with milk, honey, and spices. They baked it in hot ashes then ate the insides like pudding.

2
3/4 cup flour (175 ml)
3/4 cup whole wheat flour (175 ml)
1/2 cup wheat germ (125 ml)
1/2 cup sugar (125 ml)
1/2 cup brown sugar (125 ml)
1/2 teaspoon salt
1 teaspoon each baking soda, ground cinnamon
1/2 teaspoon each ground ginger, nutmeg, cloves

Mix together in a large bowl.
Make a deep well or crater in the center.

3
1 1/4 cups pumpkin (310 ml)

Remove seeds and cut into chunks.
Boil in water 8-12 minutes. Drain.
(Or microwave in covered dish 8 minutes.)
Purée in blender or food processor.

4
4 eggs
1/2 cup oil (125 ml)

Lightly beat eggs, then add to oil and puréed pumpkin.
Add to dry ingredients and mix just until moistened.
Spoon batter into greased mini-muffin tins.
Bake in preheated oven about 10 minutes.

Option: Add 1/2 cup (125 ml) cranberries, chopped pecans or mini chocolate chips.

Green Monster Soup

Serves 4-6

Broccoli has as much calcium as a glass of milk, more vitamin C than an orange, and more fiber than a slice of wheat bran bread.

1

2-3 large potatoes
1 small head of cauliflower
1 large onion
1 cup water (250 ml)

Chop potatoes, cauliflower, and onion.
Cook in water in large saucepan 5 minutes.

2

1 large head of broccoli

Chop broccoli and add to saucepan.
Continue to cook an additional 5-10 minutes.

3

3 cups milk (750 ml)
2 chicken or vegetable bouillon cubes
1 teaspoon Worcestershire sauce
salt and pepper to taste

Add and heat to boiling.

4

1 cup milk (250 ml)
1/3 cup flour (75 ml)
1 cup shredded Swiss or cheddar cheese (250 ml)

In small bowl, blend together milk and flour until smooth.
Stir into the soup and cook just until thickened.
Remove from heat and stir in shredded cheese.
Serve chunky or purée for a creamy soup.

Squash Mash

Serves 4-6

1

2-3 large butternut squash

Pierce squash and microwave 1-2 minutes.
Cut squash in half and remove seeds.
Peel and chop squash into large chunks.
Cover with water in large saucepan.
Boil until soft, about 20 minutes. Drain.

2

2 tablespoons butter
1 tablespoon brown sugar
1 teaspoon cinnamon
salt to taste
Combine with squash in a large bowl.
Mash with potato masher until smooth.

Option: Try another way to prepare butternut squash.
Cut squash in half lengthwise and remove seeds. Place
cut side down in shallow baking pan. Bake at 400F
(200C) 30-45 minutes until tender. Turn over and bake
until toasty brown. Add butter, honey or brown
sugar, and salt and pepper. Enjoy.

**Butternut
squash has a
sweet, nutty
taste similar to
sweet potatoes.**

Stuffed Acorns

Serves 4-6

1 Preheat oven to 350F (180C).

2 **2-3 large acorn squash**

Pierce squash and microwave 1-2 minutes.
Cut squash in half and remove seeds and strings.
Place cut side down on lightly greased baking pan.
Bake in preheated oven until almost soft, 40-50 minutes.
(Or cook in covered dish in microwave 10 minutes.)

3 **1 pound sausage** (500 g)

Sauté sausage in large frypan just until cooked.

Squash seeds have been found in ancient Mexican archaeological digs dating back to 6,000 BC.

4 **4 celery stalks**
1 medium onion
2 carrots
1/4 cup water (60 ml)
1/2 teaspoon dried sage

Finely chop celery and onion. Shred carrots.
Add vegetables, water, and sage to sausage in frypan.
Cover and simmer 15 minutes. Remove from heat.

5 **1 cup bread crumbs** (250 ml)

Mix together with sausage and vegetables.
Stuff into cooked squash halves.
Bake 10-15 minutes.

Polka Dot Pear Pancake

Serves 4

1

1 tablespoon butter

Preheat oven to 400F (200C).
While oven heats, place butter in 9-inch (1-L) pie pan and place in oven to melt.
Remove and swirl pan to grease bottom and sides.

2

1 large pear
1/4 cup cranberries (60 ml)
2 teaspoons brown sugar

Peel and thinly slice pear.
Place pear slices in bottom of pie pan on top of butter.
Dot cranberries between pears.
Sprinkle with brown sugar.

3

3/4 cup milk (175 ml)
2/3 cup flour (150 ml)
2 eggs
2 teaspoons sugar
1/2 teaspoon vanilla
1/4 teaspoon salt
1/4 teaspoon cinnamon

Whisk together in a bowl until smooth.
Pour over pears in pie pan.
Bake until puffed and golden brown, 20-25 minutes.
Remove from oven and sprinkle with powdered sugar.
Cut into wedges and serve immediately.

> The wood of a pear tree is hard enough to be made into furniture.

around the table

For the harvest time this year
We give thanks, O God.

For our garden now at rest
We give thanks, O God.

For this table filled with food
We give thanks, O God.

For our friends and family too
We give thanks, O God.

Amen.

winter

Snowflakes
drift down from the sky.
Try and catch one on your tongue.
Noses drip and cheeks grow colder
as winter blows through the yard.

Gardens painted white by snow
wait for spring to warm their soil.
Now a place for forts and snowmen
as winter crunches
underfoot.

Let's wrap up
in woolen blankets,
warm our fingers over the fire,
steaming up the frosted windows
as winter swirls around the trees.

Still our table is not empty,
filled with hardy soup and bread.
Jars of summer food sustain us.
Outside winter stakes
its claim.

winter in the garden

time to dream

In the winter the garden sleeps, mostly, while you are busy planning for spring. Draw a map of what your garden will look like— what to plant and where. Learn as much as you can about vegetables and fruits you want to plant.

When winter snows melt and the ground begins to thaw, plant seeds indoors in small containers. You can transplant the young seedlings in the garden when spring arrives.

Tools you will need:

- garden books/magazines
- notebook for ideas
- graph paper
- seed catalogs
- egg carton or containers
- potting soil
- sunny windowsill

carrot

pages 64, 67

Likes to hang out ...
alone as a crunchy snack, shredded in salad or cake, or sliced in stews and stir-fries.

Not all carrots are orange. Carrots can also come in white, red, yellow, purple, green, and black.

Grows up ...
underneath the ground. Green tops sprout above the soil with small, feathery leaves on long stems.

Ready, set, eat ...
when crisp, firm, and smooth with no splits. Choose small to medium-size carrots. Usually the brighter the carrot, the sweeter the taste.

apple

pages 64, 71

Likes to hang out ...
alone or topped with peanut butter, in salad and pie, or pressed into cider or sauce.

Grows up ...
on trees with simple oval leaves. White flowers blossom in spring and the fruit usually comes in autumn.

Ready, set, eat ...
when firm and crunchy, not soft or spongy.

Fresh apples float because 25% of their volume is air.

Look for apples with smooth, clean, shiny skin and good color. Avoid ones with cuts or bruises.

potato

Likes to hang out ... (page 67)
in creamy winter soups, cooked with cheese sauce, baked alone, mashed, or as oven fries.

Potatoes grow underground, but are actually swollen stems, not roots.

Grows up ... under the ground beneath a bushy green plant with heart-shaped leaves and blossoms of lavender or white.

Ready, set, eat ...
when the flowers drop off and the plant begins to wither. Potatoes should be firm with smooth skins and no sprouts or green spots. Potatoes are still alive when they are picked, so they should be kept in a cool area, away from the light.

sweet potato

Likes to hang out ... (page 68)
baked with butter and spices like cinnamon, in pies, as oven fries, or with black beans.

Grows up ...
under the ground with trailing vines covering the soil above.

Ready, set, eat ...
when firm and small- to medium-sized. The darker-skinned variety (often labeled as yams) with bright orange flesh are much moister when cooked than the pale-skinned sweet potato.

Sweet potatoes can be used to make flour, ink, vinegar, synthetic rubber, stamp glue, and tapioca.

beet

Likes to hang out ... (page 72)
in salads, cooked with butter, in borscht (a soup), pickled with eggs, or hiding in a cake.

Grows up ...
with a leafy green top above ground and a round root below the soil. Both the greens and the beet root can be eaten.

Beet juice is often used to color pink lemonade.

Ready, set, eat ...
when firm with a smooth skin. Smaller beets are usually more tender than large ones. If it's smaller than a tennis ball, that's good. The beet greens should be crisp and bright.

Other fruits and vegetables that store well in winter: onions, rutabagas, turnips, parsnips

63

Confetti Salad

1

1/4 cup lemon or lime juice (60 ml)
2 tablespoons orange juice
1 tablespoon honey

Mix together in a large bowl until honey is dissolved.

2

2 cups carrots (500 ml)
2 cups apple (500 ml)

Grate carrots.
Chop apples.
Add to juice mixture immediately.
(The juice will prevent the apples from turning brown.)

3

1 tablespoon fresh mint
1/8 teaspoon salt or to taste
1/4 cup raisins (60 ml)

Snip rinsed mint leaves into small pieces.
Toss with remaining ingredients and serve.

In 15th-century Europe, it was fashionable for ladies to use wild carrot flowers and leaves to decorate their hats and hair.

64

Tater Soup

Serves 3-4

1

2 tablespoons butter
1 small onion

Melt butter in large saucepan.
Chop onion and add to saucepan.
Sauté until translucent.

The "Irish" white potato that we eat today was born on a high plateau in the Andean Mountains of South America.

2

3 large potatoes
2 carrots (optional)
2 cups water or vegetable broth (500 ml)
1/2 teaspoon salt
1/4 teaspoon pepper or to taste

Peel and chop potatoes into small cubes.
Peel and chop carrots into smaller cubes or slices.
Add all to saucepan and cook about 15 minutes.

3

2 cups milk (500 ml)
3 tablespoons flour

Mix together in small bowl until smooth.
Add to soup and cook until thickened, stirring constantly.
Serve chunky or purée for a creamy soup.

Option: Turn it into cheeseburger soup by adding
1/2 lb (250 g) browned ground meat and swirling in
1 cup (250 ml) shredded cheese.

Sweet Potato Quesadillas

Serves 4-8

1 Preheat oven to 400F (200C).

2 **4 cups sweet potatoes** (1 L)

Peel and cut into large chunks.
Put in large saucepan and cover with water.
Boil until soft, 10-15 minutes. Drain.
Mash sweet potatoes with potato masher. Set aside.

3 **1½ cups onion** (375 ml)
2 cloves garlic
2 teaspoons dried oregano
1½ teaspoons each of dried basil, chili powder
1½ teaspoons ground cumin (optional)
salt and pepper to taste

Finely chop onions and garlic.
Sauté in oil in large frypan until translucent.
Add spices and cook another minute.
Stir in sweet potatoes and heat through.

4 **8 tortillas**
1 cup shredded cheddar cheese
1 cup cooked black beans (250 ml)

Spread sweet potato filling on half of each tortilla.
Spoon black beans on top and sprinkle with cheese.
Fold tortilla in half.
Place on oiled baking sheet and brush tops with oil.
Bake in preheated oven 15-20 minutes.
Serve with sour cream and salsa.

Granny Apple Rice

Serves 6

One apple tree can produce 400 apples a year.

1

1 cup brown rice (250 ml)
1¹/3 cups water (325 ml)
1 cup apple juice (250 ml)

Cook together in saucepan until tender, 40 minutes.
Set aside.

2

Preheat oven to 350F (180C).

3

1-2 tablespoons butter
1/2 large onion
1 stalk celery

Melt butter in a large frypan.
Finely chop onion and celery.
Sauté in frypan until soft.

4

2 large unpeeled Granny Smith apples
1/2 cup chopped walnuts or other nuts (125 ml)
1/4 cup brown sugar (60 ml)
1 tablespoon dried thyme or oregano
1/2 teaspoon dried summer savory
salt and pepper to taste

Dice apples.
Combine all ingredients in large bowl.
Stuff in poultry or place in casserole dish and cover.
Bake in preheated oven for 45-55 minutes.

Option: Can be topped with additional brown sugar.

Secret Chocolate Cake

Serves 12-16

1 Preheat oven to 350F (180C).

2
2 cups beets (500 ml)
1/2 cup applesauce (125 ml)

Boil beets for 20 minutes. Drain, cool, peel, and chop.
Purée with applesauce in blender. Set aside.

One third of the world's sugar supply comes not from sugar cane, but from a variety of beet known as the sugar beet.

3
11/2 cups sugar (375 ml)
1/2 cup oil (125 ml)
1/2 cup plain yogurt (125 ml)
3 eggs
11/2 teaspoons vanilla

Beat together in large mixing bowl 2 minutes.

4
11/2 cups flour (375 ml)
1 cup whole wheat flour (250 ml)
1/2 cup baking cocoa (125 ml)
11/2 teaspoons baking soda
1/2 teaspoon salt

Mix into batter with beet mixture just until blended.
Pour half of batter into greased bundt pan.

5
1 cup chocolate chips (250 ml)

Sprinkle on top of batter in bundt pan.
Pour remaining batter on top.
Bake in preheated oven 45-50 minutes.

around the table

I thank you God
For this our food
On a cold and wintery day.

I thank you God
For family, friends,
And visitors who will stay.

I thank you God
For the earth outside
Tho' quiet and still it may be.

I thank you God
For warmth inside
And the love you give to me.

Amen.

Thyme

Likes to hang out with carrots, squash, green beans, pork, poultry, or fish. Try in stuffings, soups, and cream sauces.

Basil

Likes to hang out with tomatoes and mozzarella cheese, or in pasta sauces. Pound with olive oil, garlic, pine nuts, and parmesan cheese to make pesto.

start an herb garden

Herbs are easy to grow, fun to smell, and great for cooking. All you need is a few containers, soil, and a sunny windowsill. Here are just a few herbs to get you started.

Growing: Herbs like light, open soil that drains well. Potted herbs dry out more quickly than those in the open ground, so during hot weather check the soil every day and water well.

Cutting: Clip or pick leaves often to encourage new growth. Snip the whole stem of small-leaved herbs just before flowering. Remove dead or damaged leaves and faded flowers.

Storage: Once picked, fresh herbs do not keep long. Store upright in a glass of water or wrap in a damp paper towel and store in a plastic bag in the refrigerator vegetable drawer.

Handling: When ready to use, swish in a bowl of cold water, wrap in a clean dishtowel, and shake dry. Pluck leaves from stems. Tear or snip into pieces. When cooking, add fresh herbs at the last minute for the most flavor.

Mint

Likes to hang out in fruit salads, sauces, syrups, and rich chocolate desserts. Add fresh spearmint or applemint to new potatoes, peas, and drinks.

To dry herbs:
Tie together bunches and hang them upside down in a cool, dark place. Or use your car as a dehydrator: on a sunny day, spread a layer of fresh herbs on a baking sheet and place it inside. After several hours, you'll have dried herbs and a wonderful smelling car. (You can also do the same thing in your oven at a very low temperature.) Then just crumble the leaves and store in small airtight jars.

Rosemary

Likes to hang out with lamb and pork or on top of focaccia bread. Mix with butter and add to vegetables. Strip leaves and use stems to make barbecue skewers.

Bay leaf

Likes to hang out in stews, soups, sauces, and marinades. Always remove before serving. Can also crumble dried bay leaves into potpourri.

Sage

Likes to hang out with onions in poultry stuffing, and with pork and duck. Make blended butters or cheeses. Dried sage is more powerful than fresh, so use sparingly.

Cilantro

Likes to hang out in salsa, salads, curries, stews, and chili. Cook chopped stem with beans and soups.

For cooking, 1 teaspoon of dried herbs is equal to 2-3 teaspoons of fresh herbs.

Chives

Like to hang out with eggs, salads, soft cheeses, potatoes, and sauces.

how does your garden grow?

Tending to a garden can be one of the most rewarding experiences in your life. So why not document it?

Use these pages to draw or take pictures of your fruits, vegetables, and herbs as they grow. Give them each personal names or simply call them what they are: peas, basil, strawberries. Write the date of your observation and a description of what you see—how they look, smell, and change at each stage of their lives.

At the end of the season you can look back in satisfaction and dream about next year.

1 date:
description:

1 date:
description:

2 date:
description:

2 date:
description:

3 date:
description:

3 date:
description:

1 **date:**

description:

2 **date:**

description:

3 **date:**

description:

1 **date:**

description:

2 **date:**

description:

3 **date:**

description:

1 **date:**

description:

2 **date:**

description:

3 **date:**

description:

index